I think the series is wonderful and beneficial for tourists to get information before visiting the city.

-Seckin Zumbul, Izmir Turkey

I am a world traveler who has read many trip guides but this one really made a difference for me. I would call it a heartfelt creation of a local guide expert instead of just a guide.

-Susy, Isla Holbox, Mexico

New to the area like me, this is a must have!

-Joe, Bloomington, USA

This is a good series that gets down to it when looking for things to do at your destination without having to read a novel for just a few ideas.

-Rachel, Monterey, USA

Good information to have to plan my trip to this destination.

-Pennie Farrell, Mexico

Great ideas for a port day.

-Mary Martin USA

Aptly titled, you won't just be a tourist after reading this book. You'll be greater than a tourist!

-Alan Warner, Grand Rapids, USA

Thank you for a fantastic book.

-Don, Philadelphia, USA

Even though I only have three days to spend in San Miguel in an upcoming visit, I will use the author's suggestions to guide some of my time there. An easy read - with chapters named to guide me in directions I want to go.

-Robert Catapano, USA

Great insights from a local perspective! Useful information and a very good value!

-Sarah, USA

This series provides an in-depth experience through the eyes of a local. Reading these series will help you to travel the city in with confidence and it'll make your journey a unique one.

-Andrew Teoh, Ipoh, Malaysia

>TOURIST

GREATER THAN A TOURIST – GALWAY IRELAND

50 Travel Tips from a Local

Rebecca Spelman

Greater Than a Tourist- Galway Ireland Copyright © 2018 by CZYK Publishing LLC. All Rights Reserved.

All rights reserved. No part of this book may be reproduced in any form or by any electronic or mechanical means including information storage and retrieval systems, without permission in writing from the author. The only exception is by a reviewer, who may quote short excerpts in a review.

Cover Template Creator: Lisa Rusczyk Ed. D..

Editor: Melanie Hawthorne

Image: https://pixabay.com/en/cliff-of-mohar-galway-cliff-clouds-324746/

Greater Than a Tourist
Visit our website at www.GreaterThanaTourist.com

Lock Haven, PA
All rights reserved.
ISBN: 9781981055494

>TOURIST
50 TRAVEL TIPS FROM A LOCAL

BOOK DESCRIPTION

Are you excited about planning your next trip?

Do you want to try something new?

Would you like some guidance from a local?

If you answered yes to any of these questions, then this Greater Than a Tourist book is for you.

"Greater than a Tourist- Galway" by Rebecca Spelman offers the inside scoop on Galway, Ireland. Most travel books tell you how to travel like a tourist. Although there is nothing wrong with that, as part of the Greater Than a Tourist series, this book will give you travel tips from someone who has lived at your next travel destination.

In these pages, you will discover advice that will help you throughout your stay. This book will not tell you exact addresses or store hours but instead will give you excitement and knowledge from a local that you may not find in other smaller print travel books.

Travel like a local. Slow down, stay in one place, and get to know the people and the culture. By the time you finish this book, you will be eager and prepared to travel to your next destination.

TABLE OF CONTENTS

BOOK DESCRIPTION
TABLE OF CONTENTS
DEDICATION
ABOUT THE AUTHOR
HOW TO USE THIS BOOK
FROM THE PUBLISHER
OUR STORY
WELCOME TO
> TOURIST
INTRODUCTION
1. Why Visit Galway?
2. Choosing Somewhere To Stay
3. Apps To Download Before You Leave
4. Best Times To Visit
5. Galway's Central Spots
6. Local Transport
7. Salthill
8. Cliffs of Moher
9. Places To Walk
10. Places To Eat
11. Places To Drink
12. Fancy a Snack?
13. Local Delicacies

14. Where To Buy Groceries
15. Local Markets
16. Buying Souvenirs
17. Aran Sweaters
18. Claddagh Rings
19. Nightclubs
20. Live Music
21. Best Night-Life Pubs
22. Theatre
23. NUI Galway
24. Galway Cathedral
25. The Spanish Arch
26. A Walk Along The Prom
27. The Corrib Princess
28. Hall of the Red Earl
29. Family Activities
30. The Irish Language
31. Local Phrases
32. Craic
33. Galway International Arts Festival
34. The Galway Races
35. Galway Food Festival
36. Vodafone Comedy Carnival
37. Christmas Market
38. Buskers
39. Hidden Gems

40. Local Sports
41. Finding a Public Bathroom
42. Post Office
43. Parades
44. Driving Through The City
45. Using The Euro
46. Tax-Free Purchases
47. Regular Events
48. Beach Trip
49. The People of Galway
50. Things You Should Always Carry

50 THINGS TO KNOW ABOUT PACKING LIGHT FOR TRAVEL

Packing and Planning Tips

NOTES

DEDICATION

This book is dedicated to my dogs. They can't read, but I'll make sure they know about this. It's also dedicated to my mum and dad, because they'll be annoyed if they read it and I've dedicated it to the dogs instead of them.

\>TOURIST

ABOUT THE AUTHOR

Rebecca Spelman is a writer and theatre maker who has lived in Galway since 2013, and has earned a BA in Drama, Theatre and Performance Studies with English from NUI Galway. Her first memory of Galway is falling in love with the city on a family trip when she was fifteen, and promising herself that one day, she would live there. She enjoys travelling and knows how it feels to want to explore every inch of a new place, whether or not she has enough time to do it. She has gotten to know many tourists in her time in Galway and has always been happy to help them get the most from the city she calls home. She is equally happy to help you make the most of your trip to Galway with this book, and hopes that you love the city as much as she does.

>TOURIST
HOW TO USE THIS BOOK

The Greater Than a Tourist book series was written by someone who has lived in an area for over three months. The goal of this book is to help travelers either dream or experience different locations by providing opinions from a local. The author has made suggestions based on their own experiences. Please do your own research before traveling to the area in case the suggested places are unavailable.

\>TOURIST

FROM THE PUBLISHER

Traveling can be one of the most important parts of a person's life. The anticipation and memories that you have are some of the best. As a publisher of the Greater Than a Tourist book series, as well as the popular 50 Things to Know book series, we strive to help you learn about new places, spark your imagination, and inspire you. Wherever you are and whatever you do I wish you safe, fun, and inspiring travel.

Lisa Rusczyk Ed. D.
CZYK Publishing

OUR STORY

Traveling is a passion of the "Greater than a Tourist" series creator. Lisa studied abroad in college, and for their honeymoon Lisa and her husband toured Europe. During her travels to Malta, an older man tried to give her some advice based on his own experience living on the island since he was a young boy. She was not sure if she should talk to the stranger but was interested in his advice. When traveling to some places she was wary to talk to locals because she was afraid that they weren't being genuine. Through her travels, Lisa learned how much locals had to share with tourists. Lisa created the "Greater Than a Tourist" book series to help connect people with locals. A topic that locals are very passionate about sharing.

>TOURIST

WELCOME TO
> TOURIST

>TOURIST

INTRODUCTION

Galway is a small and beautiful city nestled on the west coast of Ireland, which people from around the world come to explore thanks to its culture and welcoming atmosphere. The city is situated on the Atlantic coastline, and as such receives a lot of wind and rain, particularly in the winter. Not many people like to idly wander in such weather so if you are visiting Galway, it can be useful to know what to look out for when you arrive. Like any other city, it would take months to discover every corner of Galway worth visiting, so this book can help you find some wonderful places you might have otherwise missed. When in doubt about what to do or where to go, let Galway's charm lead you to somewhere bright and warm, where you can hear people laughing or music playing. In Galway, there are always people having fun- don't be afraid to join them!

>TOURIST

1. WHY VISIT GALWAY?

As the cultural heart of Ireland, Galway draws in many visitors due to its immersion in the arts. There are numerous festivals that take place at different points in the year, theatres which always have breathtaking shows, and street art and performances which can easily distract and enthral you as you walk through the centre. Galway is also quickly developing a reputation for its fantastic food scene- as well as annual food festivals, the city has a wide range of unique restaurants and cafes which offer delicious food with a comforting ambience. Many locals will say that a lot of the things "to do" in Galway are not activities, but rather places to congregate, eat and drink with loved ones. In this way, Galway brings people together and gives them the perfect place to reconnect with those closest to them, as well as connect with new friends. Galway is also a central spot from which you can discover many other beautiful areas that the west of Ireland has to offer, such as the Cliffs of Moher or Connemara. Spend a day exploring these wonderful places, and return to Galway for an evening dinner and a night on the town. What could be better?

2. CHOOSING SOMEWHERE TO STAY

Accommodation can be categorized according to your budget and the number of people in your group. If you are with a large group and

>TOURIST

have a low budget, a hostel may be your best choice. If your group is smaller and you would like more privacy than is offered by a hostel, searching Galway's AirBnB offerings is a great way to go. If you would like to spend a bit more and enjoy a luxurious stay, Galway has a wide range of top-class hotels in central locations throughout the city. Generally, the city centre is the best option in terms of location, but there are several suburbs such as Newcastle, Terryland, Bohermore and Westside, which are within easy walking distance of the city centre. If you are considering an accommodation option but not sure how central it is, go to Google Maps and type in the accommodation's address, then search for directions to Shop Street, Galway (this would be the most central part of the city). By doing this with each of your options, you will be able to see if some are significantly closer to the city proper than others. Hostels and hotels will have lots of information on local attractions and tours, which you are less likely to find if you book with AirBnB. However, most Galway AirBnB offerings are rooms in a local house, and many Galway AirBnB hosts regularly show their guests their favourite parts of the city, as well as taking them to events. Once again, it is purely about personal preference in terms of which accommodation option is best.

3. APPS TO DOWNLOAD BEFORE YOU LEAVE

If you are a seasoned traveller, you may already have a number of apps which you find helpful on your adventures. While not all of these apply specifically to Galway and may help you in other places, I have compiled the following list according to apps which are particularly useful in Galway:

- **Google Maps.** Before you leave home, you can search for an area, such as Galway, and download the area map to your phone, where it will stay for you to use whether or not you have an internet connection. This can be incredibly handy as you never know when you might take a wrong turn, and Google Maps will be able to give you step-by-step directions to somewhere you recognize, provided it's within the downloaded map area.

- **MyTaxi.** Galway is full of taxis, which are much more reliable than Ireland's public transport system. MyTaxi allows you to simply tap the screen to order a taxi to wherever you are, telling you exactly how long it will take the taxi to arrive. You can save your card details on the app in case you ever want to get a taxi at a time when you don't have any cash, though there is also a "pay by cash" option. MyTaxi operates throughout Europe, so it can also be a useful app if Ireland is just one of your stops on a European tour.

- **Ireland Travel Guide.** This app has information about towns and cities all over Ireland,

>TOURIST

including (of course) Galway. This is a great app to have for any Irish city as when you tap the name of the city, the app shows you a menu of all the things it can tell you about the town. Within each city, the app has information divided by the following categories:

- Sightseeing
- Eat & drink
- Nightlife
- Hotels
- Tours and shows
- Activities
- Multi-day tours
- Day trips
- City walks

Within each of these categories, you can browse through what the city has to offer, find out how to get there, and even book tickets directly from the app.

- **Galway App.** This is similar to the Ireland Travel Guide, but only contains information about Galway. It contains much the same information as the Ireland Travel Guide, but also includes information about where to find parking in the city, and the local news. This app is not as polished as its national counterpart, but it offers a more local touch. The real-time parking information is incredibly useful in Galway, and the local news and special offers are sources of information which you probably won't find in another app.

\>TOURIST

- **Deliveroo.** After a long day trip, you may return to your room and feel too tired to go into town and eat at a restaurant. That's where Deliveroo comes in! Simply type in your address, and Deliveroo will show you a range of restaurants that will deliver straight to your door. Choose what kind of food you'd like, order from the site, and wait for the food to come to you. This app can also be handy if you're hungry outside of restaurant opening times. There is a similar service with its own app called JustEat, but Deliveroo has the widest range of options and generally has a lower minimum spend amount.

4. BEST TIMES TO VISIT

As with most cities, Galway receives the majority of its visitors in the summer. While sunshine and warmth can never be guaranteed in Ireland, you are more likely to encounter it between May and September. This is also the period when many of Galway's largest events take place. The two week period in July when the Arts Festival takes place is a great time to visit, as it gives you the opportunity to experience culture from all over the world, as well as Galway's own finest offerings. The Galway Races, however, can be a less tourist-friendly event. During this week, people travel to Galway from all over the country in their thousands to watch the races and spend the evenings drinking in the town. If you are determined to visit during Race Week, I would advise that you thoroughly investigate how easy it will be to enter and exit your accommodation beforehand.

Halloween and St. Patrick's Day can also be nice times to visit Galway as the world-renowned Galway company "Macnas" put on one of their breath-taking parades in the city's streets each year. If you visit during the month of December, Galway's Christmas market will be taking place in Eyre Square, bringing some festive cheer to the city.

Each of the events mentioned here have their own section in the book, so if you would like to know more about them, just keep reading.

5. GALWAY'S CENTRAL SPOTS

When trying to find your way around the city centre, it is helpful to be aware of Eyre Square, Shop Street, and the Spanish Arch. These are three of Galway's busiest points, and are the first places a local person will mention if they are trying to give you directions. Luckily, these three spots are very close to one another. Eyre Square is a small open park surrounded by the train station, Galway shopping centre, and several banks. Just a few metres away, Shop Street begins, starting with the shop "Brown Thomas". Shop Street is a pedestrianized street combining Galway's most

>TOURIST

popular shops with historical artefacts, as well as always being populated with buskers. Once you reach the end of Shop Street, a left turn and a two minute walk will bring you to the Spanish Arch, a stone arch by the water still standing 600 years after it was built. The arch is beside another grass area where, like Eyre Square, people like to sit and take in the scenery.

Another handy spot to be aware of is the cathedral. This is on the other side of the river to the city centre, so all you need to do is cross any of the bridges you come across, and look up for the green copper dome which will guide you to this beautiful building. With these four places in mind- or marked on your map- you'll be able to find your way anywhere in Galway.

6. LOCAL TRANSPORT

Ireland's public transport system is notoriously unreliable. The two branches of public transport that cater to Galway are Bus Éireann (the national bus service) and Iarnród Éireann/ Irish Rail (the national train service). Trains are more likely to run on time than buses, but there are very few services still running. Trains are more useful for cross-country journeys, whereas buses are more likely to offer a route to nearby towns. Irish buses are very rarely on time and you if you use one, it is best to not have a tight schedule that depends on your bus arriving at its destination on time. Buses and trains both arrive and depart from Ceannt Station in Galway, which is behind the Meyrick Hotel on Eyre Square. Local buses, which all have three digit codes beginning with

>TOURIST

40 (eg. 405, 403, etc.) leave from bus stops along Eyre Square. There is another bus station, commonly known as "the new coach station"- it is even known by this name on bus timetables- which can be found two minutes away from Eyre Square. There are multiple taxi ranks at Eyre Square, as well as at numerous other points in the city. If you want fast, reliable travel within Galway, a taxi is probably the best answer.

In terms of cost , train and bus ticket prices will vary greatly depending on where you want to go, though train tickets are generally more expensive. Galway town buses charge €2.20 for an adult ticket, regardless of how far you travel. A taxi journey within the city will usually cost between €6 and €10, depending on the distance and time of day.

7. SALTHILL

A great way to see Galway's natural beauty is to walk to Salthill, then continue your walk along its promenade. This is something local people love to do, and something many do on a daily basis. Starting at the dock just across from the Spanish Arch, you simply follow the path along the coastline for about twenty minutes, taking in the view and sea breeze until you come across the little seaside town. On a sunny day, the beach is a popular place, as well as the diving board into the sea, found at the end of the promenade. The town itself is full of cute cafés, arcades, casinos, Leisureland (with mini-golf and a swimming pool), cosy pubs and restaurants, and Atlantaquaria; Galway's aquarium. Every summer, there is also a funfair set up in town, with rides and traditional funfair games. Salthill is also accessible from the main city through the 401 bus, which leaves from Eyre Square. It's the perfect place for an easy day trip.

8. CLIFFS OF MOHER

The Cliffs of Moher are situated in Co. Clare, approximately a two-hour drive south of Galway. Enjoy the picturesque view of the coastline and Atlantic Ocean, paired with the bracing wind and crash of the waves. Centuries ago, some believed that the west of Ireland was the edge of the world- as you stand at the cliffs and look out at the miles and miles of ocean, you can see how they believed that. There are numerous tour buses which directly service Galway, and will take you to and from the Cliffs, as well as bring you on a tour when you arrive there. The cliffs are part of the Wild Atlantic Way, a route along the west of Ireland which places emphasis on its most exciting areas. The Wild Atlantic Way app is a handy way to learn about the cliffs if you would rather not pay for a tour, and even includes an audio tour. The cliffs are an incredibly popular attraction, so it is advised that you book your tickets in advance to avoid disappointment. They are also likely to be wet and windy on any given day, so make sure to bring your raincoat! Guided tours can offer an informational look at this natural beauty, or you can walk along the cliffs by yourself, choosing from multiple paths. While there, many people like to visit the nearby village

>TOURIST

of Doolin and take a boat from there to the Aran Islands. These three small islands are home to picturesque views and tiny rural communities, as well as beaches and sightseeing tours.

9. PLACES TO WALK

The best-loved walk in Galway is certainly the Salthill promenade, but there are many routes which can show you the beauty of Galway- all you have to do is soak it in. If you want to walk on your own and simply observe, walking along the bay or down Shop Street and through the Latin Quarter are great. If you would like to walk all the way around Galway and see what it has to offer, there are dozens of walking tours of the city which can be booked in advance online, or booked through your local hotel or hostel. Many of these walking tours cost approximately €10 per person and focus on Galway's history, which can still be seen in the city's architecture. If you wish to go for a longer or more nature-based walk, the nearby Barna woods (approximately twenty minutes outside of the city) is a beautiful area to explore the Irish countryside without having to drive for hours.

10. PLACES TO EAT

Galway has recently blossomed into a hub for tasty food at any price, so there are a huge range of restaurants to choose from. Below, you will find some of Galway's best eateries divided into three categories: fine dining, casual, and daytime. The fine dining establishments would most closely resemble a classic restaurant;

>TOURIST

reservations may be necessary, and the price will be a bit higher than in less formal establishments. The casual eateries are perfect for last-minute plans and lower budgets, though their food is still top quality! The "daytime" places are so named because they are perfect for a tea or coffee to keep you going during a busy day, as well as a tasty breakfast or lunch. The details and addresses for each of these places can be found online.

Fine dining: Gemelle's, Cava Bodega, Aniar, Il Vicolo, Loam, Tribeton, Tulsi.

Casual: Boojum, McDonagh's, The Chili Shack, Biteclub, Dough Bros, The Pie Maker,

Pizza Napoli, Pomegranate Restaurant, Capital Kebab House, Jalan Jalan, Pasta Factory.

Daytime: Café Express, 56 Central, The Secret Garden, Renzo, Le Petit Delice, 37 West, Cupán Tae, The Jungle Café, McCambridge's, Griffin's Bakery Tea Rooms.

"I've travelled around, I've been all over this world,

Boys I ain't never seen nothin' like a Galway girl."

– Steve Earle, Galway Girl.

>TOURIST

11. PLACES TO DRINK

Like the rest of Ireland, Galway loves a drink or two. Pubs open at 11am and will close between midnight and 2am, depending on their licence. Many Irish people like to have one drink in a pub and then move on to another, so feel free to do this in order to find somewhere you like. It will also help you to see more of the city's nightlife!

If you want an old-fashioned Irish experience complete with traditional Irish music, Taafe's and Tíg Cóilí are the two best pubs. Both are located at the bottom of Shop Street, directly across the road from one another. However, due to their reputations as traditional Irish pubs, you will find a lot of tourists in both, particularly in Tíg Cóilí.

Eyre Square is a good central spot when looking for a drink, as it has a number of good pubs on and near it.

O'Connell's has an old-school traditional feel on the inside and an incredible garden out back with an old-fashioned street, bus, and pizza kitchen. Directly across the road is the Skeffington Arms, more commonly known as the Skeff. This three-storey pub features multiple bars and has a cosy feel despite its size thanks to beautiful woodwork, though its multiple levels as well as nooks and crannies, can make it a little difficult to navigate if you've had one too many. Just off Eyre Square, around the corner from O' Connell's, is

>TOURIST

An Púcán. Another large pub, it has an unusual mix of patrons of all ages, resulting in a great energy as everyone just lets go and has some fun on the dance floor.

12. FANCY A SNACK?

If you have a sweet tooth, you'll be spoiled for choice in Galway. The two most common sweet treats in Galway are ice cream and doughnuts, both of which have multiple shops selling nothing else. Depending on when in the year you visit, ice cream may not seem like your first choice. However, you're likely to spot locals eating ice cream all year around- we can't afford to wait for hot weather, so we just go for it! Gino's on Shop Street is very popular and its gelato is tasty, but it's a pretty large chain, and you'll find it elsewhere. Murphy's on High Street, however, is a Kerry-based company that is just starting to expand around the country, and their unusual flavours really reflect Ireland. They encourage you to try a taste of all their flavours before buying something, so have a go at some sea salt or brown bread ice cream- you won't regret it!

Doughnuts are very fashionable at the moment, so a number of shops selling these have popped up recently. And while many of these places sell great food, Galway's longest-standing doughnut shop is still the most interesting. Dungeons and Doughnuts on Bridge Street sells a wide array of board games, figurines and other paraphernalia, as well as sci-fi themed doughnuts. You can buy a doughnut and hot drink, rent a

>TOURIST

board game and pass the time in this one-of-a-kind shop.

If you want a savoury snack, many locals will tell you that Pizza Napoli is the place to go. Located on Cross Street, this tiny Italian restaurant sells giant individual pizza slices, costing between €3 and €4, depending on your choice of toppings. Portable and delicious, it's also a very popular choice at 2am after the pubs close.

13. LOCAL DELICACIES

As a seaside city on a small island, Galway loves its seafood just as much as you'd expect. McDonagh's on Quay Street is a hugely popular choice for fish and chips and while their food is delicious, they're so popular that you might struggle to find somewhere to sit. If you'd prefer a sit-down meal, there are some great options, such as Oscar's Seafood Bistro and Dock 1 Seafood Bar and Restaurant. Many of Galway's great seafood restaurants are right beside the docks, so you know the food will be fresh!

If you want to sample some Irish staples like lamb stew, bacon and cabbage, and all the potatoes you could want, hotels are always a great place to go. The Park House Hotel, just off Eyre Square, is a great example of home-cooked Irish classics. Many hotels offer a carvery on a daily basis, where you'll find all of the most traditional meal options.

>TOURIST

14. WHERE TO BUY GROCERIES

If you're staying in an AirBnB or just want to plan a picnic by the Cliffs of Moher, you might want to stock up on some everyday essentials. Dunnes Stores is by far the biggest supermarket in the city centre- it's located in the Eyre Square shopping centre, and you can enter it via Eyre Square or Shop Street. If you'd like a few more options, you can find Tesco, Aldi, and Lidl (three of the country's most popular supermarket chains) within two minutes' walk of one another on the Headford Road, just five minutes outside of the town. Dunnes Stores will be the most expensive, and Aldi and Lidl will be the cheapest. However, if you're looking for pre-packaged sandwiches and picnic items, Dunnes Stores and Tesco will have far more to offer.

If you run out of shampoo or need some antacids, Boots on Shop Street is incredibly useful. When you first enter it looks like it only sells makeup, but walk further into the shop and you'll find the pharmacy and its incredibly helpful staff. Boots also have a great range of travel-sized products, in case you only want to buy two or three days' worth of shower gel, rather than a big bottle.

15. LOCAL MARKETS

Galway's local markets can be a great way to find special presents and souvenirs, because they feature local, handmade products that can't be found anywhere else in the world. They also

>TOURIST

feature a lot of delicious food, so don't go on a full stomach!

The best-known market is the Galway Market, which takes place every weekend on Church Street, at the end of Shop Street beside St. Nicholas Church. This market is also open on Bank Holidays, and on Fridays in July and August. The market is open from 8am to 6pm, but many of the stalls will close before 6pm, so it's best to go early in the day to see everything.

The Flea Style Market takes place in Claddagh Hall on the last Sunday of every month, from 1 to 6pm. This is Galway's longest-running flea market, known as a great place to find interesting clothes!

The Handmade in Galway Indoor Market takes place every third Sunday in Áras na nGael, on Dominick Street. If you want to see when their next market will be, their Facebook page is the best place to go! As the name suggests, everything in this market is handmade by Galway artists. It's a great place to see beautiful work and support the local artistic community.

16. BUYING SOUVENIRS

While the local markets are wonderful places to look for souvenirs, they aren't open every day and won't have many items with catchy slogans, if that's what you're looking for. There are a large number of souvenir shops in Galway, the majority of them located on or near Shop Street. The two main items that are considered traditional Galway souvenirs are Aran sweaters and Claddagh rings, which each have their own chapter. Other than this, you will find a lot of woollen products such as blankets, hats, and scarves. You will also easily be able to find more travel-sized souvenirs, such as magnets, t-shirts and socks. Many of these shops do offer international shipping though, so don't be afraid to buy that chunky sweater or oversized wool blanket! Many of these shops have also specially trained their staff to give customers individual help and information about the products, so don't be afraid to ask when purchasing something. While it isn't generally common in Irish shops, personal customer service will be readily available in almost all of these shops.

17. ARAN SWEATERS

Aran sweaters- locally known as Aran jumpers- are something that many tourists know they want to buy when they travel to Ireland. Aran sweaters are named after the Aran Islands, where they were first made. Each family had their own pattern, and fishermen would wear their family's pattern so their bodies could be identified if they went overboard. Patterns are no longer made specifically for each family; instead, each stitch has a different meaning behind it, representing different parts of life on the Aran Islands. The Aran Islands are very small and not many people live there, so *Aran sweaters are NOT made on the Aran Islands.* If a salesperson tells you this, they are lying. You can check on the label at the bottom

\>TOURIST

of the jumper where the product was made, though many of the most popular brands (Carraig Donn, Kilronan Knitwear, etc.) were made in mainland Ireland. The name "Aran sweater" comes from the birthplace of the style and stitches, not where the sweater was made, though many companies will include the word "Aran" in their name to sound like they come from the Aran islands without actually saying they do.

Aran sweaters can be made with Aran wool, which comes from Irish sheep, but are often made with Merino wool, which comes from warmer countries. This is because Irish sheep grow up in cold, windy weather and develop much tougher, itchier wool than sheep who grow up in warmer climates. Merino wool is imported raw to Ireland

and then the products are made in Ireland. There are sweaters made from Aran wool available, but most customers find them too itchy to wear. If you have sensitive skin and find Merino wool too itchy, certain brands also make products using super-soft Merino wool which, as the name suggests, is even softer than regular Merino wool.

Another thing to note about Aran sweaters is that they are not very form-fitting. Many tourists come to Ireland expecting to find the perfect, flattering sweater, but in reality, these traditional sweaters are very loose and square-shaped. If you are looking for a more modern shape, you may have to go with a modern interpretation rather than a traditional Aran sweater.

>TOURIST

18. CLADDAGH RINGS

The Claddagh ring includes the traditional Galway symbols of two hands, a heart, and a crown. Some rings will have a gemstone on the heart, but some are entirely metal. The ring represents love (the heart), loyalty (the crown), and friendship (the hands). Local legend says it was invented by Richard Joyce in the late 17th century. There are many shops in Galway (and around the world) that sell Claddagh rings, but the original Claddagh ring shop is Thomas Dillon's Claddagh Gold. Why go anywhere else when you can get the original? This shop is located on Quay Street, and is the closest Claddagh ring shop to the Claddagh.

The way you wear your Claddagh ring is a traditional way of conveying your relationship status. For the purpose of these explanations, the direction the heart "points" is the direction in which the point at the bottom of the heart is pointing.

- Single people wear the ring on their right ring finger, pointing towards the fingertip.
- Those in a relationship wear the ring on the right ring finger, pointing towards the body.
- Engaged people wear the ring on the left ring finger, pointing towards the fingertip.
- Married people wear the ring on the left ring finger, pointing towards the body.

The reason the ring points different ways is to show that your heart is either "open" or "taken", and the rings have a long tradition of being used as engagement or wedding rings. Claddagh rings are worn by both men and women.

19. NIGHTCLUBS

If nightclubs are your thing, walk down Shop Street after about 11pm- there will be representatives from Galway's top clubs offering discount stamps. The most popular clubs in town are Electric, Carbon, 44, and DNA. Generally, it will cost you €5 or less to enter, unless there is a special event happening in that particular club, such as a guest DJ appearance. Nightclubs are very popular among students during the week, on weekends the age average goes up (usually to over 21) to cater to the non-student crowd. Both environments can be fun, but it's always good to know what to expect.

The clubs are open from 11pm to 2am- while you may be tempted to arrive early to get the most from your money, the clubs generally don't fill up until at least 11.45. There are cloakrooms for you to leave coats and bags, but you will be charged to do so. DNA offers a service to its female clients where you can buy soft flat shoes and leave your high heels in the cloakroom.

20. LIVE MUSIC

The majority of Galway's pubs have live music every weekend, if not every night. All of the pubs mentioned in previous chapters will have live music. This is the main way to listen to live music in Galway, as there are no music-only venues. The closest there would be to this would be Monroe's on Dominick Street, which has a second bar that often features live music acts, separate from its main pub and restaurant. The Róisín Dubh also features a lot of live music, but these gigs are more integrated with the rest of the pub than the events in Monroe's. Of course, you can always listen to buskers playing on Shop Street, both day and night. Some of the buskers will play on the street during the day and then in a pub that evening, so you may hear a familiar tune as you walk into a pub after a day of shopping!

"There are no strangers here, only friends that you haven't yet met."

– W.B. Yeats

21. BEST NIGHT-LIFE PUBS

For many Galway people, the night ends in the Róisín Dubh, whether or not they intend to end up there. Also known as the Róisín, this pub hosts music and comedy acts, and is well known for its silent disco every Tuesday- but it also has cosy spots and a smoking area which is famous for being a great place to have a chat. The Róisin is just around the corner from Dominick Street and across the road from Monroe's, another popular pub which features a lot of live acts.

Two other great pubs that are across the road from one another are The Front Door and Tigh Neachtain, found on Cross Street and Quay Street respectively. Both have a warm, friendly

>TOURIST

feel and are decorated with traditional items from Galway, but both also become crowded quite quickly, so you may want to go early if you want a comfortable seat!

22. THEATRE

Galway has a number of theatres that host shows all year round, as well as hosting the Galway Theatre Festival and Galway International Festival annually, which sees an increase in the shows on offer in the city. The best way to see if there are any shows worth watching while you're in Galway is to look at each theatre individually.

- **The Town Hall Theatre.** This is Galway's most central theatre, and will have more shows on than any other in town. The Town Hall hosts a wide variety of acts, from plays to musicals to dance performances.

- **Druid Theatre.** Also known as the Mick Lally Theatre, this space belongs to the world-famous Druid Theatre Company. Druid often puts on their productions in this space, as well as offering newer writers a chance to have their works read for general audiences.

- **An Taibhdhearc.** An Taibhdhearc is Ireland's national Irish language theatre, showing more productions in Irish than any other venue in the country. However, if you don't speak Irish, they may still have something for you! They also produce a number of works in English, so don't be afraid to check them out.

>TOURIST

- **The Black Box Theatre.** The Black Box on the Headford Road is the city's largest theatre, and is often used for shows which are more technically demanding, or those with a large budget. The Black Box has an incredibly wide variety of shows from season to season- you never know what will be on next!

- **Nun's Island Theatre.** This theatre is often used by the Galway Community Theatre and Galway Youth Theatre to put on regular low-cost, high-value productions. This smaller venue offers a more intimate audience experience, and is often used by different theatre companies when they want to involve the audience in the show.

- **O' Donoghue Centre.** Opened in 2017, the O' Donoghue Centre is NUI Galway's brand-new theatre building, featuring a state of the art theatre. This new theatre is used by students, faculty and alumni to create shows that display the best of what Galway's theatre community has to offer.

23. NUI GALWAY

The National University of Ireland Galway (commonly shortened to NUI Galway) is situated in the heart of Galway beside the cathedral and along the river Corrib. It has been open since 1845 and there are currently almost 20,000 students enrolled there. Due to its long history and large community, the university has long been a part of Galway's society, and Galway is often known as a "student town". Notable alumni from NUI Galway include the Irish President Michael D. Higgins, and former Taoiseach (Irish Prime Minister) Enda

>TOURIST

Kenny. The campus is open to the general public and has beautiful grounds to walk on, as well as walks along the Corrib into the countryside. The university also contains two museums; a geology museum in the Quadrangle, and a zoology museum in the Martin Ryan Building. These buildings are directly opposite of one another, so you can fit two museum trips into the one journey!

24. GALWAY CATHEDRAL

The Cathedral is officially called the Cathedral of Our Lady Assumed into Heaven & St. Nicholas. The Cathedral was built beside the river Corrib and NUI Galway in 1965, making it the youngest stone cathedral in Europe. The Cathedral was also instrumental in helping Galway receive city status. The Cathedral is open to visitors on a daily basis, asking for a voluntary donation rather than an admission fee. Visitors are welcome to attend daily Mass at 9am, 11am and 6pm on weekdays, 9am and 11am on Saturdays, and 9am, 10am, 11am, 12.30, and 6pm on Sundays. The Cathedral is also open between Mass times for visitors to come in, pray, and admire the building's beauty. The Cathedral Bookshop is located inside the building, selling souvenirs and religious books. It is possible to arrange a baptism or wedding in the Cathedral through their website.

25. THE SPANISH ARCH

The Spanish Arch is a popular meeting place for local people, especially on a sunny day when you can sit by the water and watch the

>TOURIST

world pass by. Built in 1584, the Arch is a misnomer, not actually related to the Spanish who came to Galway centuries ago at all. The Arch was built by the Eyre family and was probably known as the Eyre Arch when it was first built. Historians have guessed that the name "Spanish Arch" came from Spanish sailors docking at the edge of city and trading at the Arch, but this has not been proven. Tourists may expect something quite extravagant as the Spanish Arch is mentioned a lot by locals, however, it is simply a stone arch that is part of the old city walls. It is spoken about so much because it is a useful meeting point, rather than it being a source of entertainment. Some would say that rather than viewing the Arch as a destination, it should be considered something that enriches the journey to other destinations, such as the Galway Bay. If you walk through the Spanish Arch, you will find the Galway City Museum, which is a great (and free) source of entertainment, especially on a rainy day.

26. A WALK ALONG THE PROM

The Salthill promenade (locally called "the prom") is approximately two miles long and stretches from the Claddagh to Salthill. The prom is a perfect example of Galway's unique blend of city and country life - walk from the heart of the city to its seaside neighbour while watching the waves and admiring the mountains across the bay. Those mountains are actually the Burren, located

>TOURIST

in Co. Clare - a beautiful national park with a unique rocky landscape which creates a breathtaking sight. Walking along the prom is also a great way to get a fresh breath of sea air when it's too cold to go swimming in the sea! The Irish name for Salthill is Bóthar na Trá, which means "sea road". As you walk along the prom, you'll have the sea on one side and Galway on the other, making it a pretty picturesque journey. As you walk, you'll see others jogging, cycling, or walking children or pets; every part of the Galway community goes to the prom to get their daily exercise, and you can enjoy it with them.

27. THE CORRIB PRINCESS

The Corrib Princess is a 157-seat boat which offers daily tours down the river Corrib, through Galway's countryside and on to Lough Corrib, the largest lake in the Republic of Ireland. The boat departs from Woodquay for its ninety minute tour, passing historical and cultural sites such as castles, as well as offering breathtaking views of the local countryside. The skipper acts as a guide along this scenic tour so that you can learn all about these rare sights. This can be a great way to see the wilder natural side of the west of Ireland, and they offer Irish coffee and Irish dancing demonstrations on the boat. There are also covered and heated areas

>TOURIST

for colder, wetter days. The Corrib Princess gives tours twice a day from May to September, adding a third daily tour in July and August. The Corrib Princess is also available to book for private parties from April to October.

28. HALL OF THE RED EARL

The Hall of the Red Earl is not, in fact, a hall, but the remains of one. This fascinating archaeological site on Druid Lane is one of Galway's top tourist attractions, yet it is very rarely crowded and therefore easy to view. The site has been dated back to the thirteenth century and linked to the founding of the city of Galway by the Anglo-Normans, specifically the de Burgo family. The "Red Earl" that the building is named after is Richard de Burgo, who would have local tribesmen meet him in his hall to bend the knee to him. The hall served many purposes including hosting banquets, collecting taxes, and serving as a sort of early court, where justice was served. This hall was abandoned in the 15th century when the tribes of Galway took over the city and was only rediscovered in 1997 during the first stages of new construction. As well as the hall's foundations, numerous artefacts were found on the site, which are shown in cases along with descriptions of how they would have been used. The entire site has been beautifully preserved by a glass hall which visitors can walk through in order to get a thorough look at this marvellous piece of history.

29. FAMILY ACTIVITIES

There is a huge range of family-friendly parks and activity centres in Co. Galway but if you're looking for something within city limits, look below:

- **Soft play areas.** If your little ones are still quite young, there is a number of soft play areas in Galway and the surrounding suburbs. Kidsplace in Ballybrit, Busy Bees in Oranmore, and Monkey Business in Knocknacarra are all great options.
- **Barna Woods.** Located just three miles outside of the city, Barna Woods is a beautiful local forest, perfect for family

walks, climbing trees and playing hide-and-seek. There are also some historical points of note such as the remains of Barna Castle and the Barna Holy Well.

- **Leisureland.** Located in Salthill, Leisureland has a number of swimming pools featuring interactive water activities, an inflatable obstacle course, and a water slide. Outside, there's a crazy golf course all year round and fairground rides during the summer.

- **Planet Entertainment Centre.** This is the perfect place if you have multiple children of different ages. With a soft play area, bowling, laser tag and arcade games, you'll find something to suit everyone. The centre

>TOURIST

is located on Headford Road, less than five minutes from Eyre Square, making it the most central spot for family fun.

- **Atlantaquaria.** This aquarium in Salthill is open seven days a week and offers guided tours, fish feeding and allows you to leave and re-enter throughout the day. You can also download an exhibit guide from their website and create a personalised tour for you and your family based on what you'd like to see.

30. THE IRISH LANGUAGE

First of all, the native language of Ireland is Irish, not Gaelic. The Irish word for the Irish language is "Gaeilge" (pronounced Gale-ga or gwale-ga), but in English, it is only called "Irish". Irish is a mandatory subject in all primary and secondary schools, but very few people use it once they leave school. You are more likely to hear Irish in Galway than any other Irish city, but you still may not hear it at all. The most common place to see Irish is on signs and public information. You'll never see information in Irish that doesn't have an English translation alongside it though. The Irish for Galway is "Gaillimh" and the Irish for Ireland is "Éire" or "Éireann", which you may see on some souvenirs or clothing. You may also see signs on pubs that say "Ceol, ól agus craic"- this means "music, drink and fun", though I will give a full explanation on what exactly "craic" is in Chapter 32.

>TOURIST

"Only Irish coffee provides in a single glass all four essential food groups: alcohol, caffeine, sugar, and fat." – Alex Levine

31. LOCAL PHRASES

Below are a few phrases which you may hear locals say. You are, of course, free to use these words and phrases in Galway if you wish, but you will not be taken seriously if you do.

- **Well.** Hello.

- **What's the craic?** What's up/ how are you?

- **Grand.** Fine/good.

- **Loveen.** A term of endearment, usually used towards women.

- **Sham.** A friend, or someone who thinks highly of themselves.

- **Lush.** Alcoholic drink.

- **Feen.** Man.

- **The jacks.** Toilet.

- **Wrecked.** Tired (sometimes after a night out).

- **The guards.** The police- this comes from the Irish word for police, gardaí (pronounced guard-ee)

- **Sparch.** The Spanish Arch.

32. CRAIC

"Craic" (pronounced "crack") is a very commonly used word in Ireland. You'll see it written on souvenirs and pub signs, hear people ask each other "What's the craic?" and give "For the craic" as the reason for doing pretty much anything. "Craic" is an Irish word and its closest equivalent in English is "fun", but it isn't a perfect

>TOURIST

translation. If you haven't been to Ireland before, you might only fully understand what craic is when you get here and meet the people. Irish people are known around the world for being fun-loving and carefree, and that's the key to craic; doing something fun just because it's fun. Craic is a very important part of Irish life and culture- it gives the people their easygoing attitude and allows them to have the fun they're so well-known for. When you're in Ireland, don't overthink things- just have a bit of craic!

33. GALWAY INTERNATIONAL ARTS FESTIVAL

The Galway International Arts Festival runs for two weeks every July (usually the last two weeks of the month) and had its 40th festival in 2017. The Arts Festival has been instrumental in cultivating Galway as a cultural hub, and brings hundreds of thousands of visitors to the city every year. The festival showcases dozens of acts and events over the two week period from theatre shows and live music to art installations and street performances. Artists and companies travel to Galway from all over the world to take part in this internationally-acclaimed event. No matter what kind of thing you like, the Arts Festival will have something for you. The festival gives people the

>TOURIST

opportunity to see art forms that aren't as popular or easy to find, such as dance or spoken word. There are also large-scale events such as street parades and the Big Top concert, which has featured acts such as Passenger, Bon Iver, and Joni Mitchell in the past.

The festival encourages not only attending artistic events, but discussing them. Many of the performances conclude with a discussion or Q&A, encouraging people to come together as a community and bond over their shared love for the arts. The Arts Festival is a great place for those who make art and those who appreciate it to meet, giving everyone involved a richer experience.

Tickets can be bought from the GIAF website, as well as from a kiosk in Eyre Square or by calling the venue of an individual show. There are many Festival volunteers in the town over the two weeks to offer guidance, and timetables and descriptions of events are free to take in multiple places around Galway. There are also a large number of free events, so you can enjoy the Festival no matter what your budget is!

34. THE GALWAY RACES

People have been coming to Galway to watch horse racing for centuries, and there are few in Galway who haven't gone to the races at least once. The high point of this is Race Week, which takes place every summer at the end of July and beginning of August. Over 150,000 people attend the races over this week, and Galway is full to the brim of visiting race-goers.

>TOURIST

A lot of people who attend the Races come primarily for the social aspect, and for events such as Ladies' Day, where the best dressed lady wins a prize. The races take place in the nearby suburb of Ballybrit, but many people stay in the city centre to enjoy a night on the town after a day of racing. This is an incredibly busy time for Galway and if you are not interested in horse racing, it may be best to delay your trip to Galway until the following week.

35. GALWAY FOOD FESTIVAL

Beginning in 2011, the Food Festival is one of Galway's newer festivals. The festival was set up to provide food education, focus on good food provenance and showcase local and international treats. It takes place in the city over the course of a week in April every year. Explore the pop-up food markets around the city, discovering new foods and inspiration for recipes to recreate at home! There are also cooking demonstrations, themed performances and fun events for the entire family to take part in. The festival is facilitated by the Galway City Museum and as such, the festival is just as much about culture, history, and community as it is about food. A great way to learn about a new place is through its food, and you can learn a lot about Ireland (and Galway) through this fun festival.

>TOURIST

36. VODAFONE COMEDY CARNIVAL

There's a lot of stand-up comedy in Galway all year round in venues such as the Roisin Dubh and The Cellar, but every October, the Vodafone Comedy Carnival comes to town and has everyone crying with laughter. The festival runs for a week at the end of October and features over fifty shows. Its acts are a mixture of Irish and international stars, and tickets sell out quickly as a lot of the acts are well-known in the comedy industry. The venues are spread out over the town, and include the Town Hall Theatre, the Black Box Theatre, and a series of large tents are set up in Eyre Square, so that the shows are right in the heart of town. Tommy Tiernan appears at the festival almost every year, and has been previously joined by other big names in comedy, such as:

- Dara O' Briain
- The Rubberbandits
- Kevin Bridges
- Patton Oswalt
- Al Porter
- Reginald D. Hunter
- David O' Doherty
- Jon Richardson
- Katy Brand
- Foil, Arms and Hog

All of the shows start at 8pm unless otherwise stated on the ticket, which is great when you want something to do but don't want to be walking around on a cold October night. Tickets are

>TOURIST

available on the Vodafone Comedy Carnival website, but there will also be tickets available at the door of any show that isn't sold out, however if you plan to do this, just know that you may end up disappointed.

37. CHRISTMAS MARKET

The Galway Continental Christmas Market is a magical event which lights up Eyre Square and brings a rush of Christmas cheer every winter. The market runs from the 21st November to the 21st December and is open seven days a week. From Monday to Wednesday, it's open from 12pm to 8pm; from Thursday to Sunday, it's open from 10am to 10pm. The market has now become a Christmas tradition for the people of Galway, and hundreds of thousands of people attend it every year.

For the month, Eyre Square is taken over by cute little kiosks styled like wooden cabins, as well as the German Bier Keller selling German beer and seasonal drinks, a huge carousel and a Ferris wheel! Over fifty traders take part in the market, as well as a number of charities raising money and reminding us what the season of giving is really about. Here are some of the wonderful products you can expect to see at the market:

- Hot food such as pretzels, burgers and hot dogs
- Hot chocolate, mulled wine and hot cider
- Handmade Christmas decorations

>TOURIST

- Handmade crafts, sold as presents for those you love or as something special for yourself
- Lots of sweets! The "Man of Aran Fudge" stall selling local handmade fudge is a popular choice.
- Quirky presents such as pet clothing, beautiful house décor, and handmade beauty products

As well as all of this, there's a Santa's Grotto, carolling, children's workshops and charity and community events taking place almost every day. It's impossible to visit the Christmas Market and not feel the spirit of Christmas. You won't be able to wait for Santa to come!

38. BUSKERS

No matter what time of the day or night you walk down Shop Street, it's highly unlikely that you won't pass at least one busker. Ed Sheeran famously busked on Galway's streets when he was a teenager, so you may be listening to a future star! You'll find a lot of solo singers with acoustic guitars, but there are also a variety of acts such as bands, piano players, jugglers, magicians and dancers. There's no charge to watch or listen, but it's considered good etiquette to throw some change into the hat or guitar case laid out in front of the performer if you like their stuff. The large number of buskers spread throughout the city gives it a great energy, causing many visitors to

>TOURIST

ask if there's a festival taking place on the streets. There isn't - that's just Galway!

39. HIDDEN GEMS

Here are a few little things you might not hear about in any other tourist guide:

- **Boojum.** Honestly one of the best places to eat in Galway. Mexican food with fresh ingredients, fast service, and low prices-what's not to love? People from all over the world have tried it and said it's the best Mexican food they've ever had. Located just across the road from the Spanish Arch, many locals like to get a takeaway burrito and sit by the water on a sunny day.

- **Charlie Byrne's.** A beautiful bookshop selling unusual books, second-hand copies of classics, and hand-selected staff favourites, this

Galway institution is utterly charming. Allow yourself to get lost in this labyrinth of literature.

- **St. Nicholas Church.** Located on Lombard St. in the middle of the city, this beautiful church with unbelievable acoustics hosts intimate concerts on an almost daily basis. Gaze at the architecture and let the notes wash over you in this serene yet sensational venue.

40. LOCAL SPORTS

Three of Ireland's most popular sports are Gaelic football, hurling, and soccer. This is especially true on a local level. Gaelic football and hurling are both part of the GAA (Gaelic Athletic Association) and watching a match is a great way to embrace a bit of Irish culture, as well as learn about some new sports!

\>TOURIST

- **Pearse Stadium.** Located in Salthill and open since 1957, Pearse Stadium is a central part of sports in Galway. The stadium hosts both hurling and Gaelic football matches on a local and county level.
- **Eamonn Deacy Park.** This is the place to be when soccer is played in Galway! This stadium is situated on the Dyke road, less than ten minutes outside of the city. Currently used by the Galway Football Association for both matches and training, this park has been open since 1935.

"Your feet will take you where your heart is." Irish Proverb

41. FINDING A PUBLIC BATHROOM

Before you go anywhere, it can be useful to check out the Galway City Council website, as they have a map of all the public toilets in the city. There are a few in Salthill along the promenade, but there are only two in the city itself; one on Eyre Square, and one across the road from the cathedral. Obviously, this can be problematic. Very few shops (if any) have bathrooms, but there are bathrooms in the Eyre Square shopping centre, which cost a few cents to use. The majority of hotels and restaurants won't let you use the bathroom unless you are a customer, but most pubs

>TOURIST

are more relaxed about this. There is also a McDonald's on Shop Street which can easily be accessed if you can't find anywhere else to go.

42. POST OFFICE

Galway's main post office is located on Eglinton Street, just around the corner from Eyre Square and Shop Street. It is open from 9am to 5:30pm, Monday to Friday. There is also a post office in Newcastle, across the road from the university, with the same opening hours. If you want to post something on a weekend, you can buy stamps from Spar on Mainguard Street (at the bottom of Shop Street) and drop your letter into a post box- the closest one to Spar is located on the bridge beside it. If you want to post something larger than a card or letter though, you will need to take it to a post office to be weighed and sent off.

43. PARADES

As well as the numerous parades during the Galway International Arts Festival every summer, there are two annual parades which always brighten Galway's streets.

- **St. Patrick's Day.** This parade features the finest entertainment the community has to offer, including the Galway Community Circus and Macnas, Galway's internationally-acclaimed performance troupe. The parade will start at 11.30am and finish at 1pm in Eyre Square, so make sure to arrive early if you want a good view.

- **Halloween.** The annual Halloween parade is done entirely by Macnas, who choose a new theme every year and design amazing puppets and floats accordingly. The parade usually takes place one or two days before Halloween rather than on the 31st, so check their website to see exactly when the parade is each year. Most cities do very little, if anything, for Halloween and Macnas brings the perfect blend of spookiness and magic to Galway to give you a spine-tingling evening.

44. DRIVING THROUGH THE CITY

Driving through Galway is notoriously difficult and slow, and should be avoided if at all possible. However, if you do wish to drive through the city, there are a few helpful things to know:

- **Know your route.** Galway, as well as the rest of Ireland, is not always clearly signposted. Save yourself a lot of time and frustration by looking up your route *before* you get in your car; don't leave it up to your GPS.
- **One-way roads.** This is another reason to look up your route before driving. Many of the city centre's streets are one-way and your GPS may not be aware of this. There may also not be a visible sign to tell you you're at the wrong end of a one-way street.
- **Traffic.** Because of its one-way roads and old city layout, Galway's traffic builds up at multiple points throughout

>TOURIST

the day. Avoid rush hour (morning and evening) if you can. The Headford Road is one of the worst places in the city for traffic, so see if there is another way you can go before you leave.

- **Parking.** It can be difficult to find on-street parking in Galway, so a multi-storey car park is much easier. Two useful car parks are the Jury's Inn car park beside the Spanish Arch, and the Corrib Shopping Centre car park, located just off Eyre Square. Both of these car parks have an hourly charge.

45. USING THE EURO

Before you travel, make sure to inform your bank that you will be using your card abroad so that they don't suspect fraudulent activity and shut down your account. If you will be charged a lot for using your card abroad or converting from your local currency to Euro, it can be best to use cash as much as possible. However, it is important to note that not all shops will take large notes (a €50 is often the largest note a shop will accept). Not all banks in Galway have the facilities to take your local currency and exchange it for Euro, but there are a number of large banks on Eyre Square which will all be able to do this for you. Some shops will have the option to charge your card in either Euro or your local currency, so make sure to look up the exchange rate so that you can make an informed decision and get the best value on your purchases.

>TOURIST

46. TAX-FREE PURCHASES

If you are coming to Ireland from outside the European Union, you are entitled to reclaim the tax you pay on Irish goods. This facility is available for goods only, and not services or accommodation. When you buy an item in an Irish shop, 23% VAT will be included in the price that the item has been marked. You pay the full price (which includes the VAT) and then can claim approximately half of the VAT back. This can be done in one of two ways.

Card. If you are with a tour group, your guide may give you a red card and tell you to have it swiped at shops to reclaim your tax. When paying for a purchase, you simply give the card to the cashier, and they swipe it in their machine. When you go to the airport to leave the country, you swipe the card in a similar machine.

Receipt. When you make a purchase, a cashier can give you a second receipt to reclaim your tax. You fill out the necessary details on the receipt and store all of your tax-free receipts together in a tax-free envelope, which the cashier can provide for you. You fill out each of these receipts, seal them all together in one envelope, and drop it off at the airport.

Whether you use the card or receipt will depend on the shop where you are buying the product. Both methods do the same thing, but some shops use one method and some use the other. Both methods will give you the same amount of money. When you return to the airport, both the card and envelope of receipts are dropped in at the tax-free desk. If you can't find this desk, any airport employee should know where it is.

47. REGULAR EVENTS

Little Cinema. This is a monthly event that takes place in the Roisin Dubh. For just €5, you can watch a premier showcase of short films created by local artists. You may even see a Galway location you didn't previously know about, and be inspired to visit it!

PorterShed. If you're interested in technology or business, check out the PorterShed to see what events are on while you're in Galway. There's always an interesting talk or workshop on in this start-up hub located just behind Eyre Square. This might be just the thing if you're a workaholic who needs a break from sightseeing.

Theatre Room. This is a local theatre collective who puts on a show in a different location every month; just check out their Facebook page to see where their next show will be! There's always lots of laughs as well as some poignant moments, and a great sense of community in the artistic endeavour. It's free to attend, though it is asked that a voluntary contribution be made.

Silent disco. A silent disco is where you're given a pair of headphones upon entry and can switch between multiple music channels to find something that suits you. Once you've found a song, all you have to do is dance! This is a great night out for anyone with a very particular music taste and if you ever want to talk to your friends, all you have to do is slip off your headphones. The silent disco happens in the Roisin Dubh every Tuesday night and only costs €5. Every so often, the silent disco moves outside and becomes a street party, adding another element to the fun!

48. BEACH TRIP

As with any coastal area, Galway has its fair share of beautiful beaches. Salthill is the closest option and is open to swimmers as well as walkers, but here are a few more options in case you'd like a change of scenery:

Ballyloughane Beach. This picturesque beach in Renmore is less commercial than its Salthill counterpart and is the perfect place for a stroll interspersed with a bit of rock climbing. You'll have a great view of Galway bay and a bit of privacy to admire the scenery and reflect.

Silver Strand Beach. Located in Barna (which can be reached by bus or taxi), this beach is perfect for young families as its water is shallow and ithas a lifeguard during the summer months. On a sunny day, a trip to this beach and a wander around the village of Barna can make for a lovely day out.

>TOURIST

49. THE PEOPLE OF GALWAY

The city of Galway grew from a fort of the same name which was built in the 1100s and by the 1200s, the city was ruled by fourteen families known as "the tribes of Galway". These families were Athy, Blake, Bodkin, Browne, D'Arcy, Deane, Font, French, Joyce, Kirwan, Lynch, Martin, Morris, and Skerrett. The tribesmen dominated political, commercial and social life in Galway until the late 19th century. The city also flourished during this period due to its port. It was famously visited by Spanish sailors (hence the name "Spanish Arch" of the arch by the water), as well as other Europeans including Christopher Columbus.

There are now approximately 80,000 people living in Galway; 80% Irish and 20% non-Irish. A large number of people in Galway come to and from the city every year to attend NUI Galway as well as GMIT (Galway-Mayo Institute of Technology) and GTI (Galway Technical Institute). There is also a notable number of people living in Galway who visited once and moved there, claiming they couldn't stay away.

50. THINGS YOU SHOULD ALWAYS CARRY

A few useful things that you might need at an unexpected time, or don't realize you need until it's too late. An umbrella or raincoat. Layers of clothing; Irish weather changes quickly and often, so multiple layers that can be added or removed

>TOURIST

are preferable to one thick layer Cash. Sunglasses. Hand sanitizer. Tissues. A bottle of water. Portable charger

\>TOURIST

Bonus Book

50 THINGS TO KNOW ABOUT PACKING LIGHT FOR TRAVEL

Pack the Right Way Every Time

Author: Manidipa Bhattacharyya

First Published in 2015 by Dr. Lisa Rusczyk. Copyright 2015. All Rights Reserved. No part of this publication may be reproduced, including scanning and photocopying, or distributed in any form or by any means, electronic or mechanical, or stored in a database or retrieval system without prior written permission from the publisher.

Disclaimer: The publisher has put forth an effort in preparing and arranging this book. The information provided herein by the author is provided "as is". Use this information at your own risk. The publisher is not a licensed doctor. Consult your doctor before engaging in any medical activities. The publisher and author disclaim any liabilities for any loss of profit or commercial or personal damages resulting from the information contained in this book.

Edited by Melanie Howthorne

>TOURIST

Introduction

*He who would travel happily
must travel light.*

-Antoine de Saint-Exupéry

Travel takes you to different places from seas and mountains to deserts and much more. In your travels you get to interact with different people and their cultures. You will, however, enjoy the sights and interact positively with these new people even more, if you are travelling light.

When you travel light your mind can be free from worry about your belongings. You do not have to spend precious vacation time waiting for your luggage to arrive after a long flight. There is be no chance of your bags going missing and the best part is that you need not pay a fee for checked baggage.

People who have mastered this art of packing light will root for you to take only one carry-on, wherever you go. However, many people can find it really hard to pack light. More so if you are travelling with children. Differentiating between "must have" and "just in case" items is the starting point. There will be ample shopping avenues at your destination which are just waiting to be explored.

This book will show you 'packing' in a new 'light' – pun intended – and help you to embrace light packing practices for all of your future travels.

Off to packing!

Dedication

I dedicate this book to all the travel buffs that I know, who have given me great insights into the contents of their backpacks.

About The Author

Manidipa Bhattacharyya is a creative writer and editor, with an education in English literature and Linguistics. After working in the IT industry for seven long years she decided to call it quits and follow her heart instead. Manidipa has been ghost writing, editing, proof reading and doing secondary research services for many story tellers and article writers for about three years. She stays in Kolkata, India with her husband and a busy two year old. In her own time Manidipa enjoys travelling, photography and writing flash fiction.

Manidipa believes in travelling light and never carries anything that she couldn't haul herself on a trip. However, travelling with her child changed the scenario. She seemed to carry the entire world with her for the baby on the first two trips. But good sense prevailed and she is again working her way to becoming a light traveler, this time with a kid.

The Right Travel Gear

1. Choose Your Travel Gear Carefully

While selecting your travel gear, pick items that are light weight, durable and most importantly, easy to carry. There are cases with wheels so you can drag them along – these are usually on the heavy side because of the trolley. Alternatively a backpack that you can carry comfortably on your back, or even a duffel bag that you can carry easily by hand or sling across your body are also great options. Whatever you choose, one thing to keep in mind is that the luggage itself should not weigh a ton, this will give you the flexibility to bring along one extra pair of shoes if you so desire.

2. Carry The Minimum Number Of Bags

Selecting light weight luggage is not everything. You need to restrict the number of bags you carry as well. One carry-on size bag is ideal for light travel. Most carriers allow one cabin baggage plus one purse, handbag or camera bag as long as it slides under the seat in front. So technically, you can carry two items of luggage without checking them in.

>TOURIST

3. Pack One Extra Bag

Always pack one extra empty bag along with your essential items. This could be a very light weight duffel bag or even a sturdy tote bag which takes up minimal space. In the event that you end up buying a lot of souvenirs, you already have a handy bag to stuff all that into and do not have to spend time hunting for an appropriate bag.

> *I'm very strict with my packing and have everything in its right place. I never change a rule. I hardly use anything in the hotel room. I wheel my own wardrobe in and that's it.*
>
> Charlie Watts

Clothes & Accessories

4. Plan Ahead

Figure out in advance what you plan to do on your trip. That will help you to pick that one dress you need for the occasion. If you are going to attend a wedding then you have to carry formal wear. If not, you can ditch the gown for something lighter that will be comfortable during long walks or on the beach.

5. Wear That Jacket

Remember that wearing items will not add extra luggage for your air travel. So wear that bulky jacket that you plan to carry for your trip. This saves space and can also help keep you warm during the chilly flight.

6. Mix and Match

Carry clothes that can be interchangeably used to reinvent your look. Find one top that goes well with a couple of pairs of pants or skirts. Use tops, shirts and jackets wisely along with other accessories like a scarf or a stole to create a new look.

7. Choose Your Fabric Wisely

Stuffing clothes in cramped bags definitely takes its toll which results in wrinkles. It is best to carry wrinkle free, synthetic clothes or merino tops. This will eliminate the need for that small iron you usually bring along.

> TOURIST

8. Ditch Clothes Pack Underwear

Pack more underwear and socks. These are the things that will give you a fresh feel even if you do not get a chance to wear fresh clothes. Moreover these are easy to wash and can be dried inside the hotel room itself.

9. Choose Dark Over Light

While picking your clothes choose dark coloured ones. They are easy to colour coordinate and can last longer before needing a wash. Accidental food spills and dirt from the road are less visible on darker clothes.

10. Wear Your Jeans

Take only one pair of Jeans with you, which you should wear on the flight. Remember to pick a pair that can be worn for sightseeing trips and is equally eloquent for dinner. You can add variety by adding light weight cargoes and chinos.

11. Carry Smart Accessories

The right accessory can give you a fresh look even with the same old dress. An intelligent neck-piece, a couple of bright scarves, stoles or a sarong can be used in a number of ways to add variety to your clothing. These light weight beauties can double up as a nursing cover, a light blanket, beach wear, a modesty cover for visiting places of worship, and also makes for an enthralling game of peek-a-boo.

12. Learn To Fold Your Garments

Seasoned travellers all swear by rolling their clothes for compact and wrinkle free packing. Bundle packing, where you roll the clothes around a central object as if tying it up, is also a popular method of compact and wrinkle free packing. Stacking folded clothes one on top of another is a big no-no as it makes creases extreme and they are difficult to get rid of without ironing.

13. Wash Your Dirty Laundry

One of the ways to avoid carrying loads of clothes is to wash the clothes you carry. At some places you might get to use the laundry services or a Laundromat but if you are in a pinch, best solution is to wash them yourself. If that is the plan then carrying quick drying clothes is highly recommended, which most often also happen to be the wrinkle free variety.

14. Leave Those Towels Behind

Regular towels take up a lot of space, are heavy and take ages to dry out. If you are staying at hotels they will provide you with towels anyway. If you are travelling to a remote place, where the availability of towels look doubtful, carry a light weight travel towel of viscose material to do the job.

15. Use A Compression Bag

Compression bags are getting lots of recommendation now days from regular travellers. These are useful for saving space in your luggage when you have to pack bulky dresses. While packing for the return trip, get help from the hotel staff to arrange a vacuum cleaner.

Footwear

16. Put On Your Hiking Boots

If you have plans to go hiking or trekking during your trip, you will need those bulky hiking boots. The best way to carry them is to wear them on flight to save space and luggage weight. You can remove the boots once inside and be comfortable in your socks.

17. Picking The Right Shoes

Shoes are often the bulkiest items, along with being the dainty if you are a female. They need care and take up a lot of space in your luggage. It is advisable therefore to pick shoes very carefully. If you plan to do a lot of walking and site seeing, then wearing a pair of comfortable walking shoes are a must. For more formal occasions you can carry durable, light weight flats which will not take up much space.

18. Stuff Shoes

If you happen to pack a pair of shoes, ensure you utilize their hollow insides. Tuck small items like rolled up socks or belts to save space. They will also be easy to find.

Toiletries
19. Stashing Toiletries

Carry only absolute necessities. Airline rules dictate that for one carry-on bag, liquids and gels must be in 3.4 ounce (100ml) bottles or less, and must be packed in a one quart zip-lock bag. If you are planning to stay in a hotel, the basic things will be provided for you. It's best is to buy the rest from the local market at your destination.

>TOURIST

20. Take Along Tampons

Tampons are a hard to find item in a lot of countries. Figure out how many you need and pack accordingly. For longer stays you can buy them online and have them delivered to where you are staying.

21. Get Pampered Before You Travel

Some avid travellers suggest getting a pedicure and manicure just the day before travelling. This not only gives you a well kept look, you also save the trouble of packing nail polish. Remember, every little bit of weight reduced adds up.

Electronics
22. Lugging Along Electronics

Electronics have a large role to play in our lives today. Most of us cannot imagine our lives away from our phones, laptops or tablets. However while travelling, one must consider the amount of weight these electronics add to our luggage. Thankfully smart phones come along with all the essentials tools like a camera, email access, picture editing tools and more. They are smart to the point of eliminating the need to carry multiple gadgets. Choose a smart phone that suits all your requirements and travel with the world in your palms or pocket.

23. Reduce the Number of Chargers

If you do travel with multiple electronic devices, you will have to bear the additional burden of carrying all their chargers too. Check if a single charger can be used for multiple devices. You might also consider investing in a pocket charger. These small devices support multiple devices while keeping you charged on the go.

24. Travel Friendly Apps

Along with smart phones come numerous apps, which are immensely helpful in our travels. You name it and you have an app for it at hand – take pictures, sharing with friends and family, torch to light dark roads, maps, checking flight/train times, find hotels and many other things. Use these smart alternatives to traditional items like books to eliminate weight and save space.

I get ideas about what's essential when packing my suitcase.

-Diane von Furstenberg

>TOURIST

Travelling With Kids

25. Bring Along the Stroller

Kids might enjoy walking for a while but they soon tire out and a stroller is the just the right thing for them to rest in while you continue your tour. Strollers also double duty as a luggage carrier and shopping bag holder. Remember to pick a light weight, easy to handle brand of stroller. Better yet, find out in advance if you can rent a stroller at your destination.

26. Bring Only Enough Diapers for Your Trip

Diapers take up a lot of space and add to the weight of your luggage. Therefore it is advisable to carry just enough diapers to last through the trip and a few for afterwards, till you buy fresh stock at your destination. Unless of course you are travelling to a really remote area, in which case you have no choice but to carry the load. Otherwise diapers are something you will find pretty easily.

27. Take Only A Couple Of Toys

Children are easily attracted by new things in their environment. While travelling they will find numerous 'new' objects to scrutinize and play with. Packing just one favorite toy is enough, or if there is no favorite toy leave out all of them in favor of stories or imaginary games.

28. Carry Kid Friendly Snacks

Create a small snack counter in your bag to store away quick bites for those sudden hunger pangs. Depending on the child's age this could include chocolates, raisins, dry fruits, granola bars or biscuits. Also keep a bottle of water handy for your little one. These things do not add much weight and can be adjusted in a handbag or knapsack.

29. Games to Carry

Create some travel specific, imaginary games if you have slightly grown up children, like spot the attractions. Keep a coloring book and colors handy for in-flight or hotel time. Apps on your smart phone can keep the children engaged with cartoons and story books. Older children are often entertained by games

>TOURIST

available on phones or tablets. This cuts the weight of luggage down while keeping the kids entertained.

30. Let the Kids Carry Their Load

A good thing is to start early sharing of responsibilities. Let your child pick a bag of his or her choice and pack it themselves. Keep tabs on what they are stuffing in their bags by asking if they will be using that item on the trip. It could start out being just an entertainment bag initially but with growing years they will learn to sort the useful from the superfluous. Children as little as four can maneuver a small trolley suitcase like a pro- their experience in pull along toys credit. If you are worried that you may be pulling it for them, you may want to start with a backpack.

31. Decide on Location for Children to Sleep

While on a trip you might not always get a crib at your destination, and carrying one will make life all the more difficult. Instead call ahead to see if there are any cribs or roll out beds for children. You may even put blankets on the floor. Weave them a story about camping and they will gladly sleep without any trouble.

32. Get Baby Products Delivered At Your Destination

If you are absolutely paranoid about not getting your favourite variety of diaper or brand of baby food, check out online stores like amazon.com for services in your destination city. You can buy things online ahead of your travel and get them delivered to your hotel upon arrival.

33. Feeding Needs Of Your Infants

If you are travelling with a breastfed infant, you save the trouble of carrying bottles and bottle sanitization kits. For special food, or medications, you may need to call ahead to make sure you have a refrigerator where you are staying.

34. Feeding Needs of Your Toddler

With the progression from infancy to toddler, their dietary requirements too evolve. You will have to pack some snacks for travelling time. Fresh fruits and vegetables can be purchased at your destination. Most of the cities you travel to in whichever part of the world, will have baby food products and formulas, available at the local drug-store or the supermarket.

35. Picking Clothes for Your Baby

Contrary to popular belief, babies can do without many changes of clothes. At the most pack 2 outfits per day. Pack mix and match type clothes for your little one as well. Pick things which are comfortable to wear and quick to dry.

36. Selecting Shoes for Your Baby

Like outfits, kids can make do with two pairs of comfortable shoes. If you can get some water resistant shoes it will be best. To expedite drying wet shoes, you can stuff newspaper in them then wrap them with newspaper and leave them to dry overnight.

37. Keep One Change of Clothes Handy

Travelling with kids can be tricky. Keep a change of clothes for the kids and mum handy in your purse or tote bag. This takes a bit of space in your hand luggage but comes extremely handy in case there are any accidents or spills.

38. Leave Behind Baby Accessories

Baby accessories like their bed, bath tub, car seat, crib etc. should be left at home. Many hotels provide a crib on request, while car seats can be borrowed from friends or rented. Babies can be given a bath in the hotel sink or even in the adult bath tub with a little bit of water. If you bring a few bath toys, they can be used in the bath, pool, and out of water. They can also be sanitized easily in the sink.

39. Carry a Small Load Of Plastic Bags

With children around there are chances of a number of soiled clothes and diapers. These plastic bags help to sort the dirt from the clean inside your big bag. These are very light weight and come in handy to other carry stuff as well at times.

Pack with a Purpose

40. Packing for Business Trips

One neutral-colored suit should suffice. It can be paired with different shirts, ties and accessories for different occasions. One pair of black suit pants could be worn with a matching jacket for the office or with a snazzy top for dinner.

41. Packing for A Cruise

Most cruises have formal dinners, and that formal dress usually takes up a lot of space. However you might find a tuxedo to rent. For women, a short black dress with multiple accessory options will do the trick.

42. Packing for A Long Trip Over Different Climates

The secret packing mantra for travel over multiple climates is layering. Layering traps air around your body creating insulation against the cold. The same light t-shirt that is comfortable in a warmer climate can be the innermost layer in a colder climate.

Reduce Some More Weight

43. Leave Precious Things At Home

Things that you would hate to lose or get damaged leave them at home. Precious jewelry, expensive gadgets or dresses, could be anything. You will not require these on your trip. Leave them at home and spare the load on your mind.

44. Send Souvenirs by Mail

If you have spent all your money on purchasing souvenirs, carrying them back in the same bag that you brought along would be difficult. Either pack everything in another bag and check it in the airport or get everything shipped to your home. Use an international carrier for a secure transit, but this could be more expensive than the checking fees at the airport.

45. Avoid Carrying Books

Books equal to weight. There are many reading apps which you can download on your smart phone or tab. Plus there are gadgets like Kindle and Nook that are thinner and lighter alternatives to your regular book.

Check, Get, Set, Check Again

46. Strategize Before Packing

Create a travel list and prepare all that you think you need to carry along. Keep everything on your bed or floor before packing and then think through once again – do I really need that? Any item that meets this question can be avoided. Remove whatever you don't really need and pack the rest.

47. Test Your Luggage

Once you have fully packed for the trip take a test trip with your luggage. Take your bags and go to town for window shopping for an hour. If you enjoy your hour long trip it is good to go, if not, go home and reduce the load some more. Repeat this test till you hit the right weight.

48. Add a Roll Of Duct Tape

You might wonder why, when this book has been talking about reducing stuff, we're suddenly asking you to pack something totally unusual. This is because when you have limited supplies, duct tape is immensely helpful for small repairs – a broken bag, leaking zip-lock bag, broken sunglasses, you name it and duct tape can fix it, temporarily.

49. List of Essential Items

Even though the emphasis is on packing light, there are things which have to be carried for any trip. Here is our list of essentials:

- Passport/Visa or any other ID

- Any other paper work that might be required on a trip like permits, hotel reservation confirmations etc.
- Medicines – all your prescription medicines and emergency kit, especially if you are travelling with children
- Medical or vaccination records
- Money in foreign currency if travelling to a different country
- Tickets- Email or Message them to your phone

50. Make the Most of Your Trip

Wherever you are going, whatever you hope to do we encourage you to embrace it whole-heartedly. Take in the scenery, the culture and above all, enjoy your time away from home.

On a long journey even a straw weighs heavy.

-Spanish Proverb

>TOURIST

>TOURIST

Packing and Planning Tips

A Week before Leaving

- Arrange for someone to take care of pets and water plants
- Stop mail and newspaper
- Notify Credit Card companies where you are going.
- Change your thermostat settings
- Car inspected, oil is changed, and tires have the correct pressure.
- Passports and id is up to date.
- Pay bills.
- Copy important items and download travel Apps.
- Start collecting small bills for tips

Right Before Leaving

- Clean out refrigerator.
- Empty garbage cans.
- Lock windows.
- Make sure you have the right ID with you.
- Bring cash for tips.
- Remember travel documents.
- Lock door behind you.
- Remember wallet.
- Unplug items in house and pack chargers.

Read other Greater Than a Tourist Books

Greater Than a Tourist San Miguel de Allende Guanajuato Mexico: 50 Travel Tips from a Local by Tom Peterson

Greater Than a Tourist – Lake George Area New York USA: 50 Travel Tips from a Local by Janine Hirschklau

Greater Than a Tourist – Monterey California United States: 50 Travel Tips from a Local by Katie Begley

Greater Than a Tourist – Chanai Crete Greece: 50 Travel Tips from a Local by Dimitra Papagrigoraki

Greater Than a Tourist – The Garden Route Western Cape Province South Africa: 50 Travel Tips from a Local by Li-Anne McGregor van Aardt

Greater Than a Tourist – Sevilla Andalusia Spain: 50 Travel Tips from a Local by Gabi Gazon

Greater Than a Tourist – Kota Bharu Kelantan Malaysia: 50 Travel Tips from a Local by Aditi Shukla

Children's Book: Charlie the Cavalier Travels the World by Lisa Rusczyk

> TOURIST

Visit Greater Than a Tourist for Free Travel Tips
http://GreaterThanATourist.com

Sign up for the Greater Than a Tourist Newsletter for discount days, new books, and travel information:
http://eepurl.com/cxspyf

Follow us on Facebook for tips, images, and ideas:
https://www.facebook.com/GreaterThanATourist

Follow us on Pinterest for travel tips and ideas:
http://pinterest.com/GreaterThanATourist

Follow us on Instagram for beautiful travel images:
http://Instagram.com/GreaterThanATourist

> TOURIST

Please leave your honest review of this book on Amazon and Goodreads. Please send your feedback to GreaterThanaTourist@gmail.com as we continue to improve the series. Thank you. We appreciate your positive and constructive feedback. Thank you.

\>TOURIST

NOTES

Made in United States
Orlando, FL
30 September 2023